Cocker Spaniels
Show Off

Sabrina Lakes

Sporting Dogs
FETCH MASTERS
Show Off

xist Publishing

Check out all of the books in the Fetch Masters Series

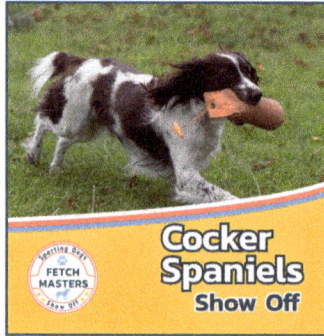

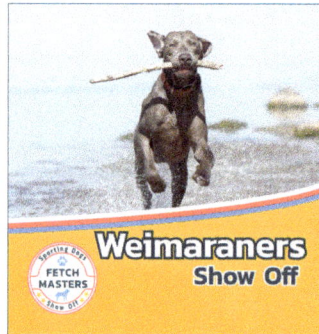

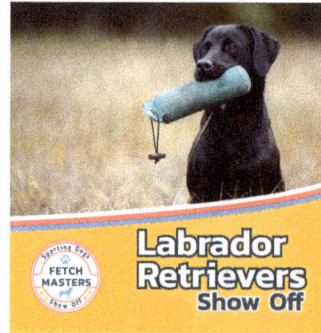

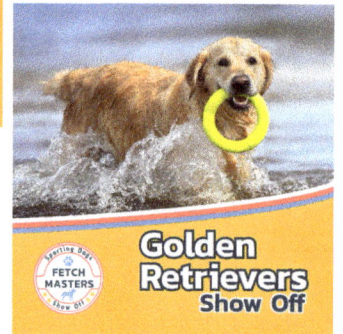

Published in the United States by Xist Publishing
www.xistpublishing.com
© 2025 Copyright Xist Publishing

First Edition
Hardcover ISBN: 978-1-5324-5519-3
Paperback ISBN: 978-1-5324-5520-9
eISBN: 978-1-5324-5518-6

PUBLISHED IN TEXAS

Table of Contents

Introduction to Cocker Spaniels

Cocker Spaniels are small to medium-sized dogs. They have long, silky fur and big, bright eyes. These dogs come from Spain, where they were bred to help hunters. Cocker Spaniels are friendly and love to be around people. They enjoy running and playing outdoors. Cocker Spaniels are also smart and learn quickly, making them great companions and working dogs.

Fun Facts About Cocker Spaniels

Cocker Spaniels have long ears that help them pick up more scents by trapping smells and guiding them toward their nose. This makes them very good at sniffing out birds and tracking their location. Cocker Spaniels come in two breeds: American and English. Both types love to play and work hard. Their fur can be many colors, like black, brown, or white. Cocker Spaniels are known for their happy and playful personalities.

What is Sporting?

Sporting means helping hunters find and bring back birds. Cocker Spaniels are great at finding small game like birds. They use their noses to sniff out where the birds are hiding. Once they find a bird, they help the hunter bring it back. Sporting dogs like Cocker Spaniels are fast, alert, and always ready to play.

Why Cocker Spaniels are Great Sporting Dogs.

Cocker Spaniels are great sporting dogs because they are energetic and love to work. They have strong noses that help them find birds quickly. Cocker Spaniels are also gentle and careful. They carry the birds softly in their mouths without damaging them. Their small size helps them move easily through thick grass and bushes.

Training a Cocker Spaniel

Training a Cocker Spaniel can be fun and rewarding. Start with simple commands like "sit" and "come." Use treats and praise to reward good behavior. Cocker Spaniels love to learn, but they can get distracted easily. Keep training sessions short and exciting. Practice every day to help your dog learn new skills.

Games to Help Cocker Spaniels Learn

Games are a great way to train Cocker Spaniels. Play fetch to teach them to bring things back. Hide treats around the house for them to find. This helps them use their noses and their brains. You can also play "hide and seek" with their favorite toy. These games make learning fun and help Cocker Spaniels stay active.

Day in the Life of a Sporting Cocker Spaniel

Cocker Spaniels start their day full of energy. They eat breakfast and get ready to work. They join hunters in the fields, running through the grass. Their noses help them find birds hiding in the bushes. Cocker Spaniels are always excited to help out and are ready for action.

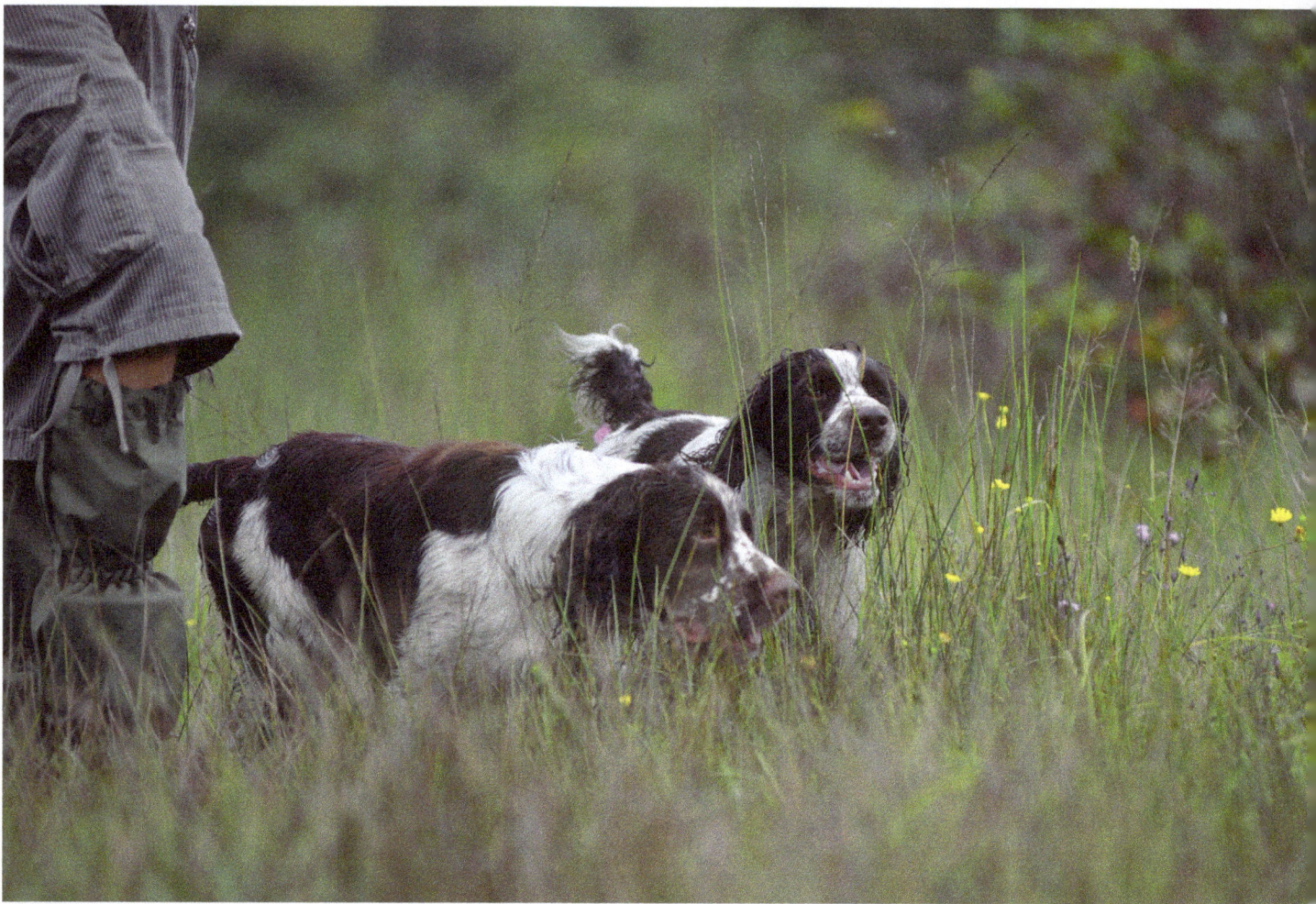

Working with the Team

Cocker Spaniels work well with hunters and other dogs. When they find a bird, they alert the hunter and gently bring it back. Their quick movements help them find and return birds quickly. Cocker Spaniels are proud of their work and love being part of the team.

Caring for a Cocker Spaniel

Cocker Spaniels need healthy food to stay active. They eat two meals a day. Brushing their fur keeps it soft and shiny. Since their ears are long, they need to be cleaned often to stay healthy. Cocker Spaniels also need their nails trimmed to help them walk comfortably.

Keeping Your Cocker Spaniel Healthy

Exercise is very important for Cocker Spaniels. They love to play, run, and explore every day. Regular walks, playtime, and games keep them happy and fit. Regular check-ups with the vet also help keep Cocker Spaniels healthy. They love to be active and spend time with their families.

Cocker Spaniels at Rest

After working hard, Cocker Spaniels need to rest. They enjoy naps in cozy places and love cuddling with their families. Rest helps them get ready for the next day. Cocker Spaniels are happiest when they are with their loved ones.

Relaxing After a Day of Work

After working hard, Cocker Spaniels need to rest. They enjoy naps in cozy places and love cuddling with their families. Rest helps them get ready for the next day. Cocker Spaniels are happiest when they are with their loved ones.

Glossary

Birds
Small game that Cocker Spaniels are trained to find.

Breeds
Different types of dogs, like American and English Cocker Spaniels.

Commands
Words used to tell a dog what to do, like "sit" or "stay."

Grooming
Taking care of a dog's fur and nails to keep them clean and healthy.

Scotland
The country where Golden Retrievers were originally bred.

Hunters
People who catch or kill animals for food or sport, often with the help of dogs.

Sporting
A category of activities or jobs that involve hunting or retrieving.

Training
The process of teaching a dog how to follow commands and perform specific tasks.

Retrieving
The action of bringing something back, specifically referring to the task that Cocker Spaniels perform by fetching birds or other items for hunters.

Index

Keyword List

Nouns	Verbs	Adjectives	Adverbs
bird	bring	alert	actively
cocker spaniel	eat	bright	carefully
command	fetch	busy	daily
day	find	careful	easily
ears	guide	energetic	eagerly
exercise	groom	excited	excitedly
family	help	friendly	gently
field	hide	gentle	happily
fur	jump	happy	quickly
game	learn	hardworking	softly
grass	move	healthy	
hunter	play	long	
mouth	rest	playful	
nose	return	proud	
scent	reward	quick	
team	run	silky	
toy	search	smart	
treat	sniff	soft	
vet	train	strong	
work	work	small	

Sporting Dogs

FETCH MASTERS

Show Off

www.ingramcontent.com/pod-product-compliance
Lightning Source LLC
LaVergne TN
LVHW070835080426
835508LV00031B/3469

9781532455209